every riven thing

poems by

Amrita Skye Blaine

Finishing Line Press
Georgetown, Kentucky

every riven thing

I dedicate this book to two poets and their unwavering support:

Fran Claggett Holland *invited me to the Blue Moon Collective before I understood I was a poet, and has encouraged and guided me for the last eight years.*

Peter Levitt, *whom I first met in graduate school twenty-three years ago, works with me one-on-one. He has brought his patience, skill, and no-nonsense style to reviewing my poems, and is a delightful mixture of kind and blunt. Our work feels like a master class, and I'm deeply grateful.*

Copyright © 2025 by Amrita Skye Blaine
ISBN 979-8-88838-970-6 First Edition
All rights reserved under International and Pan-American Copyright Conventions. No part of this book may be reproduced in any manner whatsoever without written permission from the publisher, except in the case of brief quotations embodied in critical articles and reviews.

ACKNOWLEDGMENTS

Without my skillful and attentive poetry critique group, the Blue Moon Collective, I doubt I would have found the courage to make my work public. We spur each other on!

Special thanks and love to my husband, Boudewijn Boom, who, although he is not drawn to poetry himself, listens to my poem each morning and makes thoughtful and helpful comments.

And to Rupert Spira and Elias Amidon, my spiritual teachers, who have informed and deepened my life.

I want to thank these journals and anthologies for publishing my work:

"turn toward" was published by the *New English Review*
"breath" was published by *The Merton Seasonal*
"camaraderie," "moon bathing," and "the bridge" were published in *Phases*,
    the Redwood Writers 2023 poetry anthology
"retreat hut" was published by *Soul Forte*
"singing bridge" was published by *Cold River Press*
"toy squeaks" was published by *Cold River Press*

Thank you to Elias Amidon for the phrase "love and dust" in the poem "bone house."

Publisher: Leah Huete de Maines
Editor: Christen Kincaid
Cover Art: depositphotos.com—the kintsugi image
Author Photo: Jean Porter
Cover Design: Elizabeth Maines McCleavy

Order online: www.finishinglinepress.com
            also available on amazon.com

Author inquiries and mail orders:
Finishing Line Press
PO Box 1626
Georgetown, Kentucky 40324
USA

Table of Contents

every riven thing.. 1

home

singing bridge... 4
his fuzzy self 5
dream flight 6
stripes 7
companion... 8
wonder stone... 9
retaining wall considerations 10
toy squeaks 11
moon bathing... 12

embodiment

the stain that we are.. 14
the teacher 15
on fire 16
riveting... 17
turn toward.. 18
broken 19

the work

deep snarls 22
unscathed... 23
traveler 24
when I forget 25
enter at your own risk 26
the native stream... 27
thorn... 28
tumblers... 29
Qawwali tears.. 30
subtraction... 31
the force 32
what if.. 33
eavesdropping 34
open me 35
if.. 36
because... 37
bloom with laughter.. 38
missed it... 39
daily practice 40
re-routing... 41
the bridge... 42
remade 43

questions and suggestions

productions of time 46
resilience 47
revelation 48
late-life heartbreak... 49
one prayer 50
new day 51
sponge hole heart sutra... 52
strip me 53
simpler 54
their song.. 55
the key... 56
as it is... 57
from darkness 58
your heart can bloom 59
clean ache 60

aging

harvest 62
paring down 63
our friend 64
feast 65
hymn 66
as forever 67
how it is... 68

awe

bone dance 70
the doorway 71
province 72
touchstone 73
about time... 74

silence

this, too 76
rhythm 77
love at first light 78
dumbstruck 79
late evening 80
the echo 81
nighttime canopy 82
let silence speak 83
Dervish turn 84
huge silence 85
and there I rest 86
sky walk 87
retreat hut 88
breath 89

every riven thing

looking around
it all seems bruised—
maimed from inception
yet I still hold hope
of a loving outcome
it may seem futile
but I cup it in my hand
a fragile swallowtail of faith
bold black markings on
dandelion yellow

that's why I read novels
but never thrillers
there's enough negligence
and worse right here
dealt out on a daily basis
our world straight on
starvation   murder   fires
but riven hearts radiating love—
piercing light pours
through the cracks like suns
generous and free

home

singing bridge

1953

as tires sped over
the roadway grate
the bridge—
my span home—
opened into song
cherished canticle
a psalm
soothing my way

on quiet days
I could hear it
from our house
the rhythmic chant
lub dub
at the start
a singing verse
dub lub
at the end

the city tore it down
progress, they said
the bridge
forever stilled
yet seventy years on
my heart still rings
with its song

his fuzzy self

he darted
around the oak
then up,
swiveled and stared—
he, upside down
as though the easiest feat,
a squirrel in a suave black suit,
an old woman in motion,
we eyeballed each other—
tugged from thought,
captivated right here
by his sleek, shiny self
my mouth made an O
I've never seen his kind
decked out in charcoal
his tail flicked and danced
he started and stopped
paw poised,
as though ready to flee
then settled in for
proper consideration—
his thoughtful eyes
did he see
menace or friend?
I saw friend

dream flight

I sailed over
the apple trees
their leaves
tickling my legs

the scent
of overripe fruit
under, over,
around

tilting my arms
in the humid air
I swept past
the field, cruised

over our home
waved at my sister
dipped and surged
through the sky

the ephemeral
faded, but
decades later
I remember

the light
and spacious
power
of flight

stripes

he waddles his way
through the garden
flat and wide, two
alabaster stripes
sleek and shiny
on his ink-black body,
skinny white blaze
on his ebony face
his little blunt nose,
the flicking tail
threaded with white—
he has a plan
he's on the move

I shudder as I recall
our curious old collie
skunked
by the likes of him
five days before
she died, how
she pushed through
the dog door, intent
on her mission
wiping her oily body
this side then that
onto every carpet
she could find

companion

when I was young
less than ten,
a wolf showed up
by my left side

a phantom female
sleek and tough
she sat with me
and nosed my hand
I'll walk with you
through good and hard
when you have need,
dig fingers in my ruff
and take my strength

many times I've turned,
dug my hand into her pelt
to keep me strong—
seventy years on
she's guards me still
sentinel
and friend

wonder stone

she rests on my desk
cedar green, flat
and smooth
tumbled for weeks
with coarse to fine grits
she acquired high polish
tiny pits on one side

when I'm anxious
or can't find a word,
my hand reaches
to finger the stone
my thumb loving the flaws
searches them out
like a friend in a crowd

stone, cool to the touch,
her smoothness so soothing
the pits make me pause,
take a breath—
why *she*?
that cool sensation
of Mom's hand
on my young fevered brow

retaining wall considerations

in appreciation of my husband's skill

with your engineer's eye
you stand back
take in the slope
and the fence behind
consider your approach
in silence, walk away
it's time to stew

when your work's
complete, stones fit
the earth so well
they frame the hill
it's confounding
to imagine what the land
looked like before

repeat four times
eventually, a plan
the build begins
you shape the land
smooth the ground
lay base
for your first stone

over the days
the wall takes form
you stand back
considering again
where you've been
and what you've done
that tells you
what's next to come

there are always surprises
excavating for a wall
your trowel hits
concrete buried deep
it sets you back
but not for long

toy squeaks

by my desk chair
rhythmic squeaking
my un-housetrained pup
is gnawing her soft
five-pointed star
the fourth dog to work it
she discovered the squeaker
last night in her crate
at the foot of the bed
smart girl

no starman at bedtime

my rhythm's been broken
and quiet shattered
I'll write with distraction
until she matures—
but here is the upside
she's a sweet cuddlebug
I'll trade some months
of disorder
for a decade of affection

moon bathing

rare as an oriole sighting
late-night soaks
in full moonlight
warm steam rising
a delicious seduction

when my fingers
become raisins
I climb out of the tub
into the nip of night's chill
wrap in my fleece robe
pull up the hood
to keep the heat close
to claim moonlight's touch

bathed in its grace
I slide under the covers
offer up prayers
and slip into deep sleep
that kiss of night
in the tenderest light
marks and heals me

embodiment

the stain that we are

Life, like a dome of many-coloured glass
Stains the white radiance of Eternity
—Percy Bysshe Shelley, verse 52 from "Adonais"

from the first
we have been a stain
on eternity
stain is not bad
it's light made distinct
split into spectrum
appearing as separate—
that's embodiment

caught by the mind
we fell right into
the separation trap
step back
take a breath
retrace
see what's true
we are kin of all
even earwigs
consider that

the teacher

catapulted onto stone
I can't speak
and barely breathe
there's an invitation
let pain be pain
the piercing
lie-still-on-the-ground
wait-to-see-what-happens
or, let the mind get busy
building stories into suffering
—pain *and* torment—
far worse than finding
the thread of breath again
accepting help
and staying only
here, in the warm sunshine
on unforgiving rock
head cradled in my
husband's precious hands

on fire

she borrowed an arm for a lifetime
attached to a body, of course
near the end of its tenure
now hounded with heat
the wrist is a livid bonfire
flames lick and curl inside
coals glow red in the shoulder
white pill for muscles and tissue
red-and-white capsule
for jangling nerves—
they only buff edges

the urge to push pain away
turns it into a "thing"
she draws it close, yes
lets it be what it is,
precious and tender
a near-and-dear friend
melding titanium and tissue
it's busy in there
she dives deep under pain
finds primal sensation
the clean tingle of being alive

riveting

Pain is a riveting object of attention; to paraphrase Samuel Johnson, it concentrates the mind wonderfully. —Gavin Harrison

nerve pain
shooting through
my lower back
a scouring
that empties mind
of anything
but itself—a kind
of humbling
concentration

mind wants to resist
run from pain
of course
yet here it is,
by its presence
already welcomed—
take pills
yes, call the doctor,
then move closer

edge right
into the heart
of this intimate friend
now ... nearer still
enter the pounding
pulsing rage of it
stay riveted
until it dissolves—
sheer sensation
repeat   repeat

turn toward

body parts ache
neck, head, back—
there is only dawn,
birdsong,
and the discomfort
of being alive
I turn toward it
past resistance
to welcome this,
this very morning,
none other,
to find
the secret's secret
living under, inside—
delight
in simply being
here

broken

shattered wrist
hand bone snapped
heartbroken twice
low back fracture
busted shoulder,
even stubbed toes—
watch out for walnut shells,
a few cracked molars
but most important,
broken open
bird readying for flight
the vast wide sky

the work

deep snarls

a weaver will know
that snarls in yarn
beg for slow hands—

our task, to untangle
the clump at the root

finger the knot, roll it
to soften, ease it loose
then stop.

go stand in the garden
smell the moist soil
watch a house finch
snag seed
let your heart rest

now,
return to the work
look closely—can
you tease out an end,
does it go under
or over or around?
don't touch, not yet

then act with care
be kind to yourself
thread by thread, pick
it out, see it through

unscathed

kindness is required
there's injury, pain
life is a slog
each minutia
a class in attention

he makes the mocha
she knocks it over
floods the counter
rivers the drawer
spatters oak floor
one-handed, she
snatches the laptop
out of the wave
unscathed

chance for harsh
words—none
blame doesn't happen
they work in tandem
she *I'm sorry*
he *no need*
they remake the mocha

traveler

from the outside
I seem tame
more homebody
than nomad—
trekking the South Pole
doesn't pull

the inner beckons
that little-known land
where pilgrims roam—
no suitcase to pack
no maps required
though the locale
might call for a friend

there are caves to explore
mountains, twists
and cul-de-sacs
to maneuver
until at the end
of hope
where desire
ceases there comes
a portal
to pass through, alone

when I forget

that the whole world is holy,
and tighten my circle of concern—
this summer, no monarchs
on the fuchsia, or goldfinch
pecking sunflower, only
half the songbirds I'm used to
and gophers are ruling

I need to stroll   note
redwood frond shadows
playing on the fence
riotous bush sage's spill
of soft purple velour
cedar rosettes dropping
on the patio   glorious
autumn everywhere
and then I remember

enter at your own risk

did we agree
to slip into this world
wet with fluids of love?
it's not safe, this plane—
all will be taken back
in time

in time, the one marvel
divided into many
that can sense
the interplay, though
the price we must pay
is our leaving

leaving what or where?
it's all here—
the one become many
become one
the eternal parade
of change

change is the given
no point resisting
let's rest in its river,
the pull of unknown,
give it up, let it go
float back home

the native stream

a different hunger
keeps me here—
a fox laps the birdbath,
dainty, its wildness
tamed by thirst

I, too am tamed,
framed by language
and culture
a hidden terrain
largely overlooked

but the skin
I grew into shaped
by midwestern locale
marked me
as domesticated

I long to break out,
shed my life habitat
reclaim my wildness,
drink from
the native stream

thorn

the wound
doesn't bleed
but the rosebud
embedded
its armor

it throbs

she sucks her thumb
then locates a needle
cures it in spirits
bites on her lip
and digs
the whole thorn
needs to come out
or will fester

so it is with
misunderstanding
knife deep
but with care
the full root
must be plucked
or else it regrows
and could claim her

tumblers

when the gateways
all line up,
when I feel safe
and seen,
that sawtooth edge,
the life-shaped key,
clicks tumblers
one two three…
channels clear
love is freed
to flow with ease—
the magic trick,
the sleight-of-hand
not to lock again

Qawwali tears

taught to swipe
my tears away, flick
them to the ground
rage or grief
delight, love
distinction didn't matter

a *Qawwali* friend
suggested
don't dismiss them
honor the gift they are
rub them in
with love instead
tentative, I tried

I remember
that first time
smoothing tears—
warmth toward them
changed my life
my view
this messiness
this untapped well
I make it welcome here

subtraction

God is not found in the soul by adding anything, but by a process of subtraction. —Meister Eckhart

subtraction is the key
a world to unlearn
my beliefs fell away
of who I am
and what I know
in shock
I watched them fall
I had to drop
my view of love
too personal
far too small

the concept of time
the idea of control
both had to go
time—needed
but untrue
it's always, only now—
and there is no personal
agency to manipulate,
I'm just one
tiny moving part
in this vast
and splendid whole

I'm never done
there's always more
to let go and see through
but I sense the ground
reliable and true

the force

All shall be well. And all shall be well and all manner of things shall be well ... for there is a force of love ... that holds us fast and will never let us go. —Julian of Norwich

I get blue
caught in worry
yet I remember
love
like gravity
binds us
a deep blessing

you can deny
or forget
and suffer instead
or turn toward it
welcome the force
allow it
to enter you
inviting
uplifting
sustaining

surrender
give over
your whole being
whatever the price
inside is the gift
made especially
for you
the treasure
the pearl

what if

I've spent my days
on the *what-if* train—
sometimes life
doles out worse
sometimes better
often arbitrary
always unexpected

mind grabs
the what-if convoy
like a pup
gnaws a shoe—
it knows better
but the groove,
slick with grease
of the familiar, calls—
mind chooses
the known
even as it hurts
after all,
it hurts so good

girl, step away!
try the empty
unknown—greet
the morning's chill
as a wonder
leave stories aside
must he really die
ten thousand times?

eavesdropping

have you eavesdropped
on yourself? watched
your meddling mind?
from my hinterlands
I can report that it's
a wayward place

thoughts arrive and leave
without warning
some are savage—
wanting to sting those
who stung me—
but, if I don't grab on,
don't choose
to make them mine
those thoughts
wash away

I watch them go
in the evanescent space,
that precious emptiness,
there is opportunity

open me

1986

I did not know
open me
a friend gave
this prayer
to carry in retreat—
the words
in a foreign tongue
did not frighten me
at first

until I knew
their force
open me
the sharp sword
of repetition
a blade of love
that carved a track
into my heart
drew blood
and drained
what festered there

I went home changed
not just the words—
attentive
how I use them
piercing acupuncture
heart medicine
open me

if

if I accept
the butterfly's
delicate flutter
alters
this world

if a tremble
a mere shiver
powerful
as man's war
ignites a shift

if I know this
in the deepest
heart of myself,
then it's plain
we're one vast body

and the movement
of love in my
small realm
matters

because

because dawn has opened
whether I want it or not
and I'm anxious,
a tight braid of worry

I sit still, take a breath
and sigh
this too, this life
broken open by love

I can love even me,
locked into rebuffing
what is here now
I'm a friction, a shield

because I can see this
my posture softens
I shake loose my limbs
and walk into the day

bloom with laughter

so many bumps
in the road
craters, too—
there are times
I get caught
shaken and rattled—
so what can I do?

soothe a friend's
blues, mop up
spilled stew,
gravy leaking wide
walk the dog who insists
pull apart bickering kids
wander into the garden
throw back my head
and roar
laughing—

I feel eyes upon me
a squirrel hovers nearby
unsure paws folded
as he stares—
giggles escape me
beyond my control
it's life's consolation

missed it

I missed first light
stubbed off the watch
that rumbles me awake
nodded back asleep—
this day's dawn
is gone
a minuscule thing
but a loss

a chiding whisper
lazybones
whose voice is that?
gone forty-five years
my father come to visit—
and this, his first dispatch?
then I remember
sticks and stones
can break your bones
but words
can never hurt you

useful, but not true
unless you construct
a fortress—
I whisper back
with the warmth
my heart holds,
I love you, too—
all this
from missing dawn

daily practice

most poems limp in lumpy
there may be a line
with a trace of truth
I pare dead words away—
the verse has a life
independent of mine
what does it want to say?

I repeatedly speak it,
ear for its musical echo
rephrasing a line
prune this, cut that

once in a while
it's too disheveled
for shaping—I'll snag
one single phrase
let go of the rest
and start fresh again

the rarest of poems
pours in clear—
I lift my hands
from the keys
no fussing with this one
let it shine its own song

re-routing

is this the path of love?
I ask
many times a day
when I note disquiet
has taken root

I catch myself
and remember to re-route
out of spinning thoughts
that hook me
where I have no agency—
the autocrats and climate,
wars and simple
meanness that I see
play out each day

is this the path of love?
the memo for my mind
reorients, re-centers
reminds me what is good
and kind and true
it brings me here
the only place to be

the bridge

No one can build you the bridge on which you, and only you, must cross the river of life. —Friedrich Nietzsche

it didn't look
like my mother's—
so alien she
rejected
the width, breadth
and depth of what
I was building—
my way through life

the components
I chose:
piles that drove deep,
caps and bents
to spread weight,
decking for the path
girders that soared
into light

remade

have you been consumed
by the tsunami of love?
taken, rolled to shore
flayed on rocks
and ground to sand?
this is the work of love
reshaping
and remaking
stirring us back
into love's ocean
with added spice
and bouquet,
softness and grit,
until you're no longer
discerned
as discrete

questions and suggestions

productions of time

Eternity is in love with the productions of time.
—William Blake

this ...
this wild unfolding
is meant to be
just as it is,
we can rail, weep
cry out for change
change will come
and surprise us
always new
always unexpected

my pup folds her ears
and nuzzles my arm
a production of time
just like me
here for a while
leaping, dancing
and then gone
what will arise next?
what will life
create this time?

resilience

respond now
for now

not for the future
just this

meet what's here
deep breath

then another
it's enough

be supple
remain open

there's the trick
and the gift

revelation

people speak
of enlightenment
as a landing place
a space of perfection
somewhere to get

hogwash
there is no arrival
simply more deepening
and then more and more
dive deeper still

to say you've arrived
is blasphemy—
watch ego's excitement
rubbing her hands

live in not knowing
watch dawn break
into numinous light
how it graces leaf tips
clarifying our world

note how a stone wall
holds sun's heat
radiating warmth
long past sundown

baffled and curious
consider dropping beliefs
welcome the humbling
there hides revelation

late-life heartbreak

of course,
the awful griefs—
parents, friends
acquaintances

but I didn't foresee
my biggest heartbreak
would be for the earth—
songbird decline
loss of African animals
sudden oak death
and most likely,
our species—
confronted with
our blind
unresolvable grief

how to live in this dying?
heed the immediate
lacy dragonfly wings
purpling elderberries
tang of vine-ripe tomatoes
even my old aching body—

take it all in
please don't turn away
love the casualties, too
creating fresh space
for what's new

one prayer

I used to pray
for this and that
until one day
it came clear
the only prayer
is for the highest good

there's no way
I know what's best
in any situation
boundless choices
interweaving
undivided

an accident unfolds,
offering is easy
my friend gets ill,
it's tough, I crave
a certain outcome
not mine to apprehend
so I float a prayer
for highest good

and then release it
I have no explicit
influence, clinging
stalls its work
let it go
it's done

new day

I walk outside
breathe in
the cool
the fresh
the brand new dawn

I promise this—
to be carried on
the wing of love
see it all
and sail above
coasting on eddies
the breeze
beneath my wings

or like the earthworm
who eats and aerates—
make spacious
wherever I go
enlarge your life
and mine

sponge hole heart sutra

I wring soapy water
from the sponge
struck
by the marvel of holes

how sponge soaks
up nectar or goop or juice
and holds it in hollows
suspended

how worms bore tunnels
in loam so aliment and air
percolate—without openings
soil will die

hearts require hollows,
chambers like sponge
so they can fill
and squeeze and fill again

which carries me
to the shoreless shore
sponge—emptiness
sponge—form

strip me

strip me clean of worries—
our county's loss of bees
rising temps and fires
some states banning books

strip away my gun terror
and fake-news fear
while you're at it,
take self-interest, too

leave me fresh day wonder
squirrel tail a-twitch
shimmies up the feeder
gophers thrive below

light tenders the field
house sparrows flit nearby
hummingbirds sip their fill
keep me this close in

simpler

we yearn
for simpler times
the times behind us,
or so we say
I look back 100 years
seven wars,
two worldwide,
depressions twice
two plagues
what's simple there?
perhaps we point
to when we prayed
and planted
instead of diddling
with devices—
turning ground,
under fingernails,
on our brow
that rich, moist smell
of humus,
nursing seeds
until they sprout
and feed us,
helping raise
our neighbor's barn

their song

five-thirty a.m. birds
chirping full-throated,
greeting first light
beyond them
town's rumble
rubber on pavement
airplanes lumbering
into flight

what was their tiny
songbird reaction
when those loud-mouthed
engines first lifted off?
did they feel invaded?
for millions of years
the sky had been theirs
now shared
with metal-slick bullies

they did what birds do
against the thundering
ground, feed and mate
build their nests
care for young
and watch them fledge
greet every dawn
unperturbed

the key

slow to learn
I searched in things
and those I knew
for this crux, this clue
until one day
I turned around
and found
the code inside

the key matched
a slot in my heart,
and when I slipped it in
like an arrow nocked
to its bow, it fit—
my task remained
allow trust
the turn
to open me

as it is

first light flaunts mist
fingering the trees
the birds still silent
and leaves hold quite still
earth's inhale on pause,
I'm held
in the hammock of dawn
what I can do is love
what's unfolding

we call this day *Tuesday*
the calendar says *class*
I'll prepare like it's happening
yet there is no for sure
our sun could stop shining
or poles reverse places—
I am offered the gift
of not knowing—will I
resist or accept
what's revealed?

from darkness

as first light skims
the sky, I reflect
how we birth
from dark

what a shock light
must be for the infant
as her mother finally
pushes her free

the baby caught
by a stranger then
cut from her source
with a snip of the cord

dark's comfort vanished
warm sea washed away
where is her refuge now?
no wonder she cries

imagine bewilderment
as new systems begin
lungs fill and empty
for the very first time

she squints, blinks
in this startling world
filled with loud sounds
smells and sights

as she lies skin to skin
soothed by her mother's
first touch
a new passage

from darkness to light
one into two

your heart can bloom

the most important lesson
you've learned—your
heart can bloom wide
a dinnerplate dahlia
tend it with care

cuddle the broken thing
beside the road
present as breath leaves,
protect the fledgling's
first flight
watch it catch the next
eddy and soar

racking grief,
gratitude
spilling to overflow,
rage that skins
until you forgive—
all held in a heart that blooms

clean ache

it aches to be open
I'm sorry, it does
but the price
of slamming shut
is far higher

it's a clean ache,
stretching wide
rocks me
with surprise—
battening down
fits no longer
like forcing shut
a swollen door,
a crack remains

light streams through
quaff that light
your life
depends on it

aging

harvest

it's time to reap
this life's encounter
assessing
what went well
what went wrong
scores of missteps
troubled liaisons

etched on my chest
when I landed on earth
teach me
and so life did
substantial lessons
surprise quizzes
watch what you ask for

and say yes—
I'm suggesting
it's worth it
it prodded me here
to this unexpected
improbable
realm of love

paring down

old age
called it in
I didn't choose
this stage
of paring down
like or not
outgrown roles
are slipping off
like oiled coats
shed rain

it feels respectful,
rehearsal
for what's coming
when every earthly
trait is freed—
so I let jobs go
and watch them
fall
to someone new

clearing a place
for what remains,
the work that prods
me now
this work
wants space,
breadth and depth
to dive—
I must comply

our friend

I heard by text
it was abrupt
garden collapse
here and then gone

our friend laid out
on a narrow table
in a room at her home
with an altar and flowers
there but not there
made beautiful by
women who loved her
dressed in regalia
gray hair spread out

cool bare feet
too still
so free

feast

in the longer view,
a finger snap
and life is done—

savor the spread
that is yours alone
the benediction of early light
holy kiss of dusk's dying sun

share what you can
spill paint onto murals
and let words flood—

your face thrown back,
spin in spring rain
the world needs you,
your voice, your scope
none other

hymn

a close friend
struck by a
brain-stem
stroke—a
fir half-broken
still stretching
toward light

her daughters
travel to
be by her bed
it's bad, they say
will she live?
can she write?

change is the given
I know this, yet
the echo in my chest
is a hymn of both
wonder and grief

as forever

life,
spacious when young—
once seventy, years
become months,
then rush into pure
lively moments

each day I think
about death, mostly
the how, the when
will there be pain?
can I sip the awe
of not knowing?

dawn lightens,
for a breath
all is hushed—
then the squirrel
flicks his tail
as forever
moves closer
than ever

how it is

how strange to think
I've reached an age
of dying—
I would like it
to be different,
but this is how it is
friends, family
ill or failing,
one by one—
since I don't know
and can't imagine
what is right or best
I hold for highest good

when will my time
come?
no chance to choose
I'd want a vast
and orchestrated plan
but as I age,
the more I see
there is no plan
each enigmatic moment
an opulent banquet—
I put my thoughts away
choose willingness
and dine on this—
unknown's lavish spread

awe

bone dance

400-plus pounds
the claws   the claws!
the brown bear waits
in the glacial stream
watches
with hunter's poise

the salmon
surges upstream
bucks the torrent's force
called back home
it vaults the chute

paw stretches wide
a powerful swipe
she snags the sockeye—
shreds it with a bite
chunks fall back
lost to water
translucent bones
glint in sunlight

crunched and gulped
fish becomes bear

the doorway

when my breath
catches, overcome
by tiny bird prints
in fresh snow,
the marvel of an early
crocus blossom
or barn owl in flight—
this awe is a portal,
a tender merging point

I stay still
drink in the gift
let it fill
me to spillover

eternity marks me
in a way I can share—
not the story
but the overflow of grace,
the boon of mystery

province

beyond owl hoot
and raccoon's rustle
a hush
in the redwood cathedral
rooted, they breathe for you—
standing in one place
for thousands of years
without moving
this is their gift

I kneel at the river's edge
bow to the chill
tickling my lips
its taste of stone
as the trout's body
slides by
finding its way
to a cooler eddy—
scooping water
I splash my face
this, a province of wonder

touchstone

amidst news
so disturbing I
cannot watch

still
joy washes through

wonder doesn't rise
from this world—
it seeps in
from the big field
a welcome touchstone

the blessing
of a passionflower,
their five-fingered
hearts beg bees,
I unearth potatoes
soil still clinging
carrots, too, their
salmon selves slip
from their bed

I soak in this joy

about time

as a child, it crawled—
the long spread of summer
hot, humid days
the stream in the woods
where I plunged
hands into chill water
wrestled a stone
from the bottom
stared wide-eyed
at fossils, I ran
fingers over a body
millions of years old—
for the first time
I felt awestruck and small

now the days rumble by
like bumps on the road
first light, last light
first light again
urgency presses
there's work to be done
I don't hunt for fossils
or watch seedlings grow
but that awe took root—
breath in and out
words filling a page
these mark my days

silence

this, too

so tired
tired of infighting
hatred, weary of lies
we've slipped
off the diving board
what is this human
aversion to truth?
let's cherish the bowl
of our fragile home

kintsugi calls
we can mend ourselves
with rivulets of goodness
choose gold
gold lacquer and rice flour
a delicate harmony

only start
sit in silence
parse what is
right now—all of it—
the lush air

at sunup's first blush
the hawk nabs a gopher

this, too
with a slender brush
smooth liquid gold
into the seams

rhythm

the only vowel is *y*
starting with *rh*
ending with *thm*
a weird concoction
for a word
I bow to daily

the first meaning
is poetic—*prosody*
repeated pattern
measured flow
the sound is juicy
in my mouth

rise at dawn
hug my husband
cuddle the pup
then feed her
make my mocha
time to write

rhythm
chisels my day
shapes a poem
allows me to rest
in the sway
of enigma

love at first light

love pours down
in every drop   not
a lazy rain
undemanding, steady—
more than shower
less than deluge

birds come awake
in the gray   feast
on sunflower, shaking
their red-dusted wings
hunger-driven
they crowd the feeder
in the wet chill

the ground
guzzles it in
this land so dry
reservoirs sport
steep copper walls,
pleasure boats
crowding
the pocket-size lake
that remains

and isn't each drop
that pings the roof
a grace, a blessing
filling the aquifer,
wet love quenching
land's thirst?
down, down keep
pouring
this, my prayer

dumbstruck

walking nearby
hibiscus, geranium,
fruiting fig and apple,
redwoods shedding
their needles,
the brown crunch
under my feet
roses and jasmine
flavoring the air
we walk past
all kinds of dogs
little and long
smooth-coated and curly
sniffers and runners
amazed by the medley
stunned by variety
I stop
breathe in the miracle
how did this come to be?

late evening

the way it limns
eucalyptus trees
their peeling bark
glowing
in the soft, late light

my heart pauses
or is it my breath?
I stop still
dog sits at my side
good dog

but the light has me—
swept into awe
I am rooted in place
bathed in the sweet
ephemera

I resist
pulling out my phone—
a photo
won't capture
what caught me

and then
just like that
the light is gone
can't call it back
we turn for home

the echo

some dawns
I awaken,
already drunk
on the plainsong
of silence
forever here
it sings my bones
reverberates
my heart
an unending
echo of love

nighttime canopy

I shiver under stars,
head thrown back
awestruck
by the lucent night
the depth and breadth
unknown

the age of stars
long dead, they say,
yet their light flames
alive to me—
they serve as pledge
and flare
the stamina, the chain
from there to there
to here

it's said we're made
from the dust of stars
far-flung,
I stare at them
so far away
they're also made of me

let silence speak

silence is lusty
it hangs in the clouds
drifts behind rivers
hides within dovesong
even lurks inside tinnitus
we flow from it
are made of it
rest in it
return to it

sometimes it sings
sometimes growls
it often hides
gets very quiet
it will whisper to you
form it into a hammock
lie in its embrace
it won't tell you stories
but will share its secret

Dervish turn

1999

she settles her *sikke*
firmly on her head
prays it will not fall off

bows to the *Sheikh*
raises her wings—
one palm skyward
receiving grace
one palm earthward
mercy
to this mangled world
turn, turn, and turn
until everything vanishes

her circle skirt rises
soft leather slippers
kiss the ground
there is music
she does not hear it
silence settles inside

huge silence

There is a huge silence within each of us, beckoning us back into itself. —Meister Eckhart

it's always there
waiting to be noticed
the fathomless well
that calls me inward
into the heart
of the heart
I follow it down
deeper
find silence's support
how it buoys
how it thirsts,
welcoming
those who remember—
held by the depth
thankful, I bow

and there I rest

in my days
I need a breath
a pause
and in that place
that can't be touched,
find my wandering way

in the depths
the soul of heart
that keeps me true
I meet myself
both common
and unique

and there I rest
or swim or soak
until something floats
into sight, I examine it,
consider—
worthy of words?

if not, I let it loose
with kindness
and a blessing
watch it coast away
and tend with love
the opening it leaves

this space, this place
that can't be touched
that nurtures all I am
caesura
a breath   a pause
a grace

sky walk

with a toe, I test
the wire's tension
pick up my pole
transfixed
by the gorge

wire stretches
over the canyon
from this wall to that
my crossing
to make

slow my breath
steady my heart
my life to walk
I ease my foot
onto the wire

to save my own life
attention narrows
to now and here
trouble fades
as I feel my way

slide into
the unknown
I didn't choose
never
would have asked for

each life is a tightrope
a chasm below
I lift my gaze
trust my heart
and take the next step

retreat hut

I don't attend church
that stone-steepled place
my sanctuary is inside
an internal hut
I attend
on a regular basis—
not only on Sundays
in fact, I live there
rest in the big
luminous field
offer gratitude
breathe
listen
pray

breath

some take for granted
this rosary called breath
each inbreath an invocation
every outbreath a prayer
prayer in
prayer out
softest susurration

I sit in silence with
generous light returning
the robin's early song
my easy breathing—
no entreaties
no words at all

Amrita Skye Blaine grew up on Moon Valley Lane, a dead-end street high on a hill overlooking a bend in the Ohio River. She spent much of her childhood outdoors, roaming the woods, looking for fossils, begging to own a horse, and if not that, an Irish wolfhound. Her long-held dream was to become a veterinarian, until her own vet (in the late 1950s) told her it wasn't a job for girls.

Amrita wrote soppy romantic poetry as a teenager and showed it to no one. Drawn to writing, she took one of the first creative writing classes offered at university. The professor, a young, cocky guy, tore her first short story up, threw it in the wastepaper basket in front of the whole class, and quipped it was so bad, it didn't even deserve comments. She didn't write again for twenty-seven years.

In 1992, in a freak accident, she was hit by a huge falling oak branch that nearly killed her, but also cracked her open. As soon as she could creep back to her computer, she began *Bound to Love, a memoir of grit and gratitude*, the story of raising her disabled son. Quickly realizing she needed to study creative writing, she participated in WriteLab (now defunct), completing twenty-four online writing exercises which taught her the basics of creative prose. She studied fiction at the University of Oregon under the poet Robert Hill Long, who encouraged her to attend graduate school. She earned her MFA from Antioch University in both creative nonfiction and fiction in 2003. Since 2015, she has published her memoir and a trilogy of novels, *Unleashed, Must Like Dogs*, and *Passing the Torch*.

Poetry has taken over her life. Amrita writes a poem every day, and considers it her spiritual practice. This year, her poems have been published in the Redwood Writers anthology *Phases, Soul-Lit, Delta Poetry Review, Braided Way Magazine, The Merton Seasonal, MacQueen's Quinterly, Poetry Breakfast, The Penwood Review*, and the *New English Review*.

She is part of the Blue Moon Collective with Fran Claggett-Holland, Les Bernstein, and other wonderful poets. Amrita develops themes of aging, coming of age, disability, the degradation of our world, and spiritual awakening.

Amrita lives in Sebastopol, California with her husband, Boudewijn Boom, and their dog, Jazz, who often shows up in her poems.

www.ingramcontent.com/pod-product-compliance
Lightning Source LLC
Chambersburg PA
CBHW030054170426
43197CB00010B/1515